Stra...

a Scottish-based feminist publishing collective

Published by Stramullion Co-operative Ltd., 1981
43 Candlemaker Row, Edinburgh EH1 2QB.

Project Co-ordinator: Moira Turnbull, assisted by Joy Pitman
Co-Editor: Sigrid Nielsen

Typesetting by Joy Rice at Student Community Press, 30 Grindlay Street,
Edinburgh.
Printed by Paramount, Canonmills House, Canon Street,
Edinburgh

Distributed by Scottish and Northern Book Distribution Co-operative
Ltd., 48a Hamilton Place, Edinburgh EH3 5AY
and 4th floor, 18 Granby Row, Manchester M1 3GE
and by Southern Distribution, Albion Yard, 17a Balfe Street,
London N1.

ISBN 0-907343-01-5

THE RIME OF
THE ANCIENT FEMINIST

BY STEPHANIE MARKMAN

WITH ILLUSTRATIONS BY LAURA MAY

For everyone who was there

I

It is an ancient feminist,
and she stoppeth one of three.
"By thy long grey hair and piercing stare,
now wherefore stopp'st thou me?

"The conference doors are opened wide,
the women wait within;
their burning eyes, their fearful cries -
may'st hear the dreadful din."

She held her with her withered hand:
her face, her look, was bleak.
"This is a women's conference,
and I've a right to speak."

She held her with her women's sign,
as to and fro it glistened.
The woman now was mesmerised;
despite herself she listened.

The woman stood beside the hall
and never a word she missed;
and so spoke on that ancient one,
the stern-browed feminist.

"I have an image of myself
as I was at that time,
involved with all the right young men,
my prospects were sublime.

A salary, a pension scheme,
professional career,
but what I wanted for myself
was never very clear.

Too tightly tied to turn aside,
my bound feet led me through - "
The woman hissed, and clenched her fist,
for she heard the women boo.

A man is standing in the hall,
red as a rose is he.
"You want the men's, it's on the left,"
they shout sarcastically.

The women howled; the woman growled;
but never a word she missed.
And so spoke on that ancient one,
the stern-browed feminist.

"My parents didn't tumble, as
they spun me in their dreams;
the cloth they cut their daughter from
was splitting at the seams.

They told me I was just depressed,
the panic meant I needed rest;
I swallowed gladly, soon suppressed
the rage that burnt there still.
I put a lid upon myself,
and held it there with will.

But when I tried to stop the pills,
the panic came back doubled.
At last my mind cut out, though underneath
I seethed and bubbled.

And then a numbness filled me, where
the panic once had been;
I could not think, I could not speak,
I could not feel my skin.

While deep within, beyond my reach,
the rage was all around;
it clawed and bit, it hissed and spit,
and yet it made no sound.

At length did cross the man I was
to see as my preserver;
and little knowing what I did,
I hailed him with some fervour.

He patronised, he sympathised,
he knew about depression.
The mist inside me lifted as
I made each new confession.

He patronised, he sympathised,
I didn't need to think;
which made my head hurt less and thus
removed me from the brink. '

I cut the tablets down to two
and then to one a day;
I couldn't tell the difference while
he gazed at me that way."

"You scare me, ancient feminist:
your bleak look makes me shiver."
"A straw went past - I clutched it, fast -
I married my deliverer.

II

Where on occasion I have thought
safe harbour to be found,
I've seen on looking closer that
my ship has run aground.

Just so at first I only felt
relief at having landed,
but as time passed, to my dismay
I saw that I was stranded.

Although I know, at lowest ebb,
I'd hung on every word,
now parts of me were pained to see
such patronage preferred.
Beginnings of uncertainty
all faint within me stirred.

As yet these doubts were weakened by
a look, a smile, a kiss;
in other moods I couldn't see
that there was much amiss.
The voices in me whispered: there
is nothing wrong with this.

If I was so encompassed by
his circle of protection,
what need had I to mourn if I
had lost my own direction?

His loving lips to fasten mine,
his arms to hold me tight;
what matter how I spent my day,
if he'd be there at night?

Day after day, day after day,
the pale face at the curtain.
What need to move, to stir at all,
when love was still so certain?

Day after day, day after day,
too dazzled by his spell,
to see the well-worn flagstones, see
the contours of the cell.

Walls and ceilings everywhere;
I could not rise above them;
walls and ceilings everywhere,
in time I learnt to love them.

The pale face at the window,
never moving, never talking,
a figure walking in her sleep,
or sleeping in her walking.

In rows of houses, rows of women,
silent and alone;
I only knew my own constraint,
I only knew my own.

In rows of houses, rows of women,
staring into space,
a fixed expression in the eyes,
a fixed smile on the face.

A fixed expression in the eyes,
the skull's immobile grin,
all energy, all will, all spent
on holding, holding in.

I feel that weight upon me yet,
across the years it lingers;
instead of a cross about my neck,
a ring upon my fingers.

III

Now daily more confined by him,
more trapped within my head,
I nun-like clung devoted to
this saviour I had wed.
I sought my safety in his arms,
I sought it in his bed.

So insecure I must ensure
our marriage does not fail,
I turn to him at night and thus
complete my self-betrayal.

He enters me triumphantly;
I passively comply;
if it will make him love me, then
the price is not too high.

I get no pleasure from the act,
and scared that I'll destroy it,
when he will not come on his own
I shake and moan and toss and groan,
pretending to enjoy it.

I get no pleasure from the act
till later, when we nestle.
He cuddles me contentedly,
I'm happy that he's found in me
a satisfactory vessel.

When he had duly satisfied
his bride (or so he thought),
my loving husband shrank from me
and shrank from more support.

No mind for what he left behind,
interminable, grey:
his thoughts were set on higher things
than how I spent my day.
Impatiently, he'd shrug me off.
'Go see your friends,' he'd say.

Ironic, then, my warder's words
when he would grant me bail;
for though the key was offered me,
I could not leave my gaol.

Out in a crowd, my heart beat loud,
as though it meant to burst.
I knew that I would drop there if
I couldn't reach home first.

I'd flash and flash and flash with fear
till panic closed my brain.
Those feelings that I'd thought had died
once more descended on me; I'd
be in a mist again.

I feared and dreaded each new bout,
too lonely on my own;
with hordes of people on the street,
a fearful panic stayed my feet
and kept me there, alone.

Thus his was all the power; his
was all the victory:
for I could only leave the house
if he was there with me.

So much was I held in, so much
within had been confined,
I could not let myself escape
for fear of what I'd find.

And terrified of letting go,
afraid to let my madness show,
I kept myself in rein,
and struggled hard to keep control,
to outwardly fulfil my role,
act normal, safe and sane.
But though it seemed the building stood,
inside was only rotting wood,
collapsing under strain.

The rafters crumbled, timber tumbled,
props and struts destroyed;
in vain I looked inside for strength,
for all I found was void.

Now all was still and deathly silent
in my silent head.
In vain I looked inside for strength,
for all inside was dead.

I'd tried so hard to kill my fears,
I'd killed myself instead.
Now all was silent as the grave,
for all inside was dead."

IV

"I fear you, ancient feminist;
I fear your face so grim.
I fear the grinding of your teeth
each time you speak of him.

"I fear your dreadful pallor and
the dead look in your eye,
but most I fear to hear your tale -"
"Fear not! I did not die.

Alone, alone and loveless in
a barren place I dwelt,
with no-one to illuminate
the darkness that I felt.

My husband, seeing I was lost,
lost interest in me;
apparently he liked his women
brave and strong and free

and though he'd helped to make the bed
in which I had to lie,
he pulled the sheets above my head
and left me there to die.

The dead can feel no anger, though,
the dead can feel no grief.
What anger can a phantom show
when all is dead beneath?

I pushed the pain inside to where
I couldn't feel its bite,
and sank the more in lethargy,
accepting fatalistically
that he was in the right.

With nothing that I cared to do
and nowhere left to go,
for days I hardly left my chair,
but let my torpor grow.

I dammed my tears inside myself
for fear that I might drown,
thus when at last I roused myself
and dragged myself up town,
once more the panic flashed in me,
once more it dragged me down.

The phosphorescent twilight streets,
the people rushing home,
a rushing tide, and I inside,
and I inside, alone.

I saw its floodlit windows as
I shivered at the stop;
as through a fog, I saw them shimmer,
saw the lighting wink and glimmer,
looked into the shop.

Within the shadow of myself
I stared out through the blur;
made calculations painfully,
while something caged inside of me
at last began to stir.

Beyond the shadow of myself,
I stared in through the pane.
I saw the goods, the lines displayed,
I thought of what I might have paid
and stared and stared again.

I saw what I had tried to want,
what it was offered for,
I saw it as my sanity
that I could take no more;
and something caged inside of me
at last began to roar.

And as the anger flamed within,
as it began to burn,
I knew that I had left his house,
and never need return.

LAURA

V

Oh anger is a healing thing,
it cauterises pain.
The poisons deep inside of me
rose up like pus and bubbled free
and left me whole and sane.

The poisons deep inside of me
that had so long remained,
the fire burnt them clean away
and left my body drained.

Where wounds had been, where open sores,
the fire searing, healing;
the fire raged, the fire cleansed,
inflamed me into feeling.

Out of the deadly holocaust,
the ashes of the pyre,
the phoenix comes arising, and
arising, rises higher.

Out of the conflagration, from
the furnace of my fear,
a flame licked at my eyelids till
it burnt the sockets clear.

And suddenly, my liberty
was loosening my mind;
I feverishly began to read
each Marxist tome, each socialist screed,
each new text I could find.

I felt no cooling of my rage,
my anger did not pass;
instead, I re-directed it
against the ruling class.

I fuelled it more with things I read,
albeit in confusion,
and took the cause up with some zeal:
I'd champion the common weal
and fight for revolution.

My mind was wracked with facts, with tracts,
with every new demand,
though much of what I read in them
I did not understand.

And much did not relate to me
or what I had been through -
yet still, they spoke so urgently,
I knew they must be true.

If I could free the working man,
I'd be free too, thought I:
at last I could commit myself,
at last identify.
My lethargy went up in smoke;
I had no time to die.

My head was full to bursting point,
my brain was near to fission.
My mind was filled with different men
all urging their position."

"I fear you, ancient feminist!"
"Be still and fear no more!
The wrangling voices were not me,
not splitting personality,
but real men that I saw.

When evening came, they'd drop their work
and hurry to the meeting.
The chairman gave a nod to each,
a most fraternal greeting.

The scrape of chairs, the hostile stares,
the voices of dissension,
as each in turn would raise his hand
and make his intervention.

I'd sometimes listen silently,
I'd sometimes try to speak.
The comrades looked so tired and bored,
I'd get confused and overawed,
my voice would break and squeak.

I'd stammer out my phrases and
look red-faced at the floor;
the comrades waited till I'd done,
then went on as before.

Or sometimes one would sleep with me,
and when we were undressed,
and I was snuggled sleepily,
he'd suddenly suggest
a book or two that I might read
to study the oppressed.

The list was never-ending and
the pamphlets often dreary,
yet faithfully I read them all
and tried to learn the theory.

I learnt how we would change the world,
but not how we'd relate.
Increasingly I pondered on
the world we would create.
My lover said, 'There's work to do:
relationships can wait.

'The labour movement is the key;
the power of invective;
we can't waste time on sentiment,
if we're to be effective.
You're always thinking of yourself,
you're always so subjective.'

He said I must develop the
correct objective stance,
that dreaming of relationships
would hinder my advance.

It's middle-class to talk of love,
and caring is effete -
I left the room without a word,
ran down the stairs, and overheard
two women in the street.

'That's her,' said one, 'the woman who
I mentioned once to you,
was living with that awful man,
and married to him, too.

'I saw her once out shopping, and
she sounded quite bereft;
but now, it seems, she's left him
and is working with the left.'

The other had a softer voice.
She said, 'I've often found
it's bad to be judgemental, for
we none of us are sound.'

VI

First Voice

I can't help feeling critical,
on seeing such a waste;
if I can't criticise her life,
I'll criticise her taste.

Second Voice

But she who eats in slavery
may lose her appetite,
then when she's freed she'll feed and feed,
and savour every bite.

With no thought then of why or when
or what she's going to eat,
it's not until she's gorged her fill
her taste becomes discreet.

First Voice

Then she'll come to her senses, if
we let it take its course?

Second Voice

I think that she will sicken and
get fed up with their sauce.

Eventually, she'll find their line
impossible to swallow.
Just now, she's bound to serve them, but
revolt will surely follow.

She will not stomach them for long,
if I'm not wrong,' she cried.
The women passed from earshot then,
and I passed back inside.

I found the comrades in the bar,
united as one faction,
ignoring in embarrassment
my recent hasty action.

With pointed nods in my direction
as I sidled in,
they spoke of bourgeois consciousness,
of lack of discipline.

I felt my hands go trembling as
I readied for the fight,
the endless running battle over
which of us was right.

I felt my heart go hammering -
then, with a strange elation,
some new-found strength, unearthed at length,
some new determination,
I simply turned my head away,
refused the confrontation.

I felt my stomach churning, felt
the walls begin to sway;
a sullen, swelling sickness as
I turned to move away.

A sudden beading perspiration,
dank against my skin;
a sour bile ascending, raw and
acrid from within.

And moving swiftly to the door
and swiftly hurrying through,
came swiftly to the ladies' room,
came swiftly, there, to spew.

It seemed to me a triumph that
at last I'd gone too far,
imagining the horror of
the men out in the bar.

And as I swayed and bent my head
to retch and retch again,
confused impressions of the night
went spinning in my brain.

The women in the street whose faces
I had yet to see;
a shaft of moonlight through a window
falling onto me;

the comrades in the bar who talked
of women's liberation,
diversion from the struggle and
unsound preoccupation.

I straightened, wiped my streaming eyes
and rinsed my mouth out clear;
a bitter taste had lingered there
that did not come from beer.

I knew they'd still be sitting round,
detached and analytical,
as though I'd never left the room,
quite rational, quite critical;

that they as men felt threatened when
confronted by emotion,
so built great dikes of dialectic,
holding back the ocean.

Yet though they strutted, sealords, strong,
within their crumbling wall,
the rocks on which they built their church
would smash, would crash, would fall.

The artificial great divide
created by their fright
to mask and hide the moon, the tide,
could not withstand the night.

A sudden noise disrupted me;
I started from the gloom
as several figures, laughing, vital,
breezed into the room.

I recognised the voices of
the women from outside,
and rose quite shaky to my feet
as if to stand aside.

They'd brought some other women with them,
strangers to the city,
with open, rosy, sturdy looks,
not elegant, not pretty;
their faces stern, but with concern -
with anger, not with pity.

VII

They lived out in a women's house
which stood beside the shore.
I'd seen them at a meeting when
they'd said they couldn't work with men
and slammed right out the door.

They'd asked the other women there
to talk about their lives,
to speak of their experience
as daughters, mothers, wives.

I'd held back then; I held back now,
afraid of giving way,
still fearing if I gave myself
I'd give myself away.

Still standing rigid, speechless, frigid,
staring all about,
until I felt the room go swimming,
heard a woman shout:
'For god's sake get some air in here:
I think she's passing out.

'This place is really claustrophobic,
that's what's made her sick.
The window's locked, or blocked, or jammed;
let's try to get it open, and
let's get her outside, quick.'

'You're always rushing into things,'
another woman said.
'I'd always go,' the first said, slow,
'where angels fear to tread.'

Then, with a grin, 'If fools rush in,
I'll gladly play the fool.'
They laughing took me by the arm
and took me through the hall.

Across the bar I stumbled on,
with one on either side.
The door clanged shut behind my back,
I found myself outside.

I almost turned and rushed back in,
in momentary fright,
in gazing at the blazing moon,
the stark black, dark black night.
But firm and calm they kept my arm
and kept me to my flight.

My panic ebbed away, away;
the women onwards urged.
Their energy surrounded me
and through my body surged

a wave of pleasure, sweet and strong:
I stopped, I gave a moan.
I gently shook their hands from me,
and stood there on my own.

Then from the sand, there blew inland
a wind, both soft and light.
I smelt the salt smell of the sea,
and smelt it with delight
and took a mighty breath of it
and ran with all my might.

And now I stood beside the sea,
the salt tears on my cheek.
The women came and called my name,
as if to bid me speak.

The sea was washing, washing in;
beneath the moon it stirred.
I turned to share my life with them;
they took it in, they heard.

I poured it out, the pain, the doubt;
I ripped away the shell.
When I was bare before their stare,
they spoke of theirs as well.

Since then, there have been moments when
I feel it all again,
and feel compelled to speak, to tell,
to spell out all my pain.

I go to every women's centre,
every women's place:
I look into the women's eyes,
and now and then I recognise
a certain look, a face.

The women come, now one by one
they trickle through the door.
But deep within, I hear a din,
a dim and muted roar.
The sound of women's fighting hits me,
splits me to the core.

Oh sister, I have lived too long
in barren, arid lands;
a dismal place, without embrace,
without the touch of hands.

I've seen too much dissension,
too much strife, too much despair;
and still I wait to celebrate
the sisterhood we share.

To know again that all my pain
is not confined to me;
that other women share the hurt,
that though our lives take root in dirt
we still grow strong and free.

This one thing more I'll tell you, sister,
then I have to go;
if anger is our weapon, then
be careful where you throw.

If anger is our weapon,
don't ignite it showing off;
for anger is explosive, and
right now it's going off."

The woman watched her walk away,
how slow and sure she strode;
and thus, without a backward glance,
she went off up the road

and left the woman sitting there
to meditate at leisure,
to wait until her friends came through
and hug them all with pleasure.

Catalogue available from STRAMULLION

Other feminist publishers include:-

Onlywomen Press Ltd., 38 Mount Pleasant, London WC1
Sheba Feminist Publishers, 488 Kingsland Road, London E8 4AE
Virago, 5 Wardour Street, London W1V 3HE
The Women's Press, 124 Shoreditch High Street, London E1 6JE